Direct Mail Ministry

Evangelism, Stewardship, Caregiving

Creative Leadership Series

Direct Mail Ministry

Evangelism, Stewardship, Caregiving

Walter Mueller

Creative Leadership Series

Lyle E. Schaller, Editor

Abingdon Press / Nashville

DIRECT MAIL MINISTRY

Copyright © 1989 by Abingdon Press

This book is printed on acid-free paper.

Library of Congress Cataloging-in-Publication Data

Mueller, Walter, 1932-
    Direct mail ministry: evangelism, stewardship, caregiving /
Walter Mueller: Lyle E. Schaller, editor.
        p.   cm.—(Creative leadership series)
    Bibliography: p.
    ISBN 0-687-10800-4 (alk. paper)
    1. Direct-mail ministry. I. Title. II. Series.
BV653.2.M84   1989
254.3—dc19   88-34147
                                                                  CIP

MANUFACTURED BY THE PARTHENON PRESS AT
NASHVILLE, TENNESSEE, UNITED STATES OF AMERICA

To
the congregation of
Supplee Memorial Presbyterian Church (USA)

Contents

Foreword

"That would never work for us!"

Those words reflect a frequent response whenever a new course of action is proposed in any organization. That is the normal and predictable reaction to many new ideas. However, that negative response should not be viewed as rejection, but rather as "No, not yet." Sometimes people need more time to talk themselves into making a change. On other occasions the decision makers want proof that the new idea has worked elsewhere.

This book covers both of these points. The theme of the book is that direct mail is the most cost effective approach to new member enlistment available to churches. It also is the most efficient vehicle for expanding the pastoral care of the people and for expanding the financial base of the congregation. It is a method of communication that goes back to the letters of Paul.

In addition, this book also is the autobiographical testimony of a skilled pastor who has used direct mail in three different congregations. His detailed account should win over the skeptics who claim, "That would never work for us!" It offers a working model that can not only persuade the skeptics, but also convert the opposition. This is a case study of the effective use of direct mail.

The third value of this book is the lucid "how-to-do-it" explanation for implementing a new idea. In step by step terms, the author not only explains the many values of direct mail, but also leads the reader through the process of adapting the direct mail approach to a particular congregation.

A reasonable guess is that the mailings produced by churches in 1996 will bear the same resemblance to the mailings of 1981 as a Boeing 747 jetliner does to the DC3 of the 1930s. Desktop publishing is about to revolutionize parish newsletters, annual reports, and other mailings that flow out of church offices. This book is an introduction to that impending revolution in parish communications.

An obvious question is what will be the impact on the small congregation that cannot afford this technology? One answer is that few congregations can afford to ignore it. Earlier in this century most churches rejected electric lights and telephones, but they eventually concluded that these were essential. In comparative terms, the cost of installing a direct mail system in your congregation is far less than the cost of wiring a building for electricity earlier in this century. The big differences are that electricity (a) was primarily for the convenience and benefit of today's members, (b) increased annual expenditures, and (c) was part of a larger plan to bring electricity to the entire neighborhood, while direct mail can be a means (a) of reaching tomorrow's prospective new members, (b) of expanding revenues rather than simply increasing expenditures, and (c) of pioneering a new channel of communication not yet widely used by other churches in your community.

In other words, the small congregation should be looking at benefits rather than worrying about costs. For many smaller churches, the choice may be between (a) ignoring the potential values of direct mail and watching the congregation gradually grow older and smaller and utilizing the values of direct mail to enable that congregation to contact, reach, serve, attract, and assimilate a new generation of members. That choice, rather than the cost, may be the critical issue in this debate.

This is one of several books in the CREATIVE

LEADERSHIP SERIES, designed to challenge local church leaders with innovative approaches to ministry that can broaden a congregation's outreach beyond its own members. We hope it will help you expand the ministry and outreach of your congregation.

LYLE E. SCHALLER
Yokefellow Institute
Richmond, Indiana

Introduction

Jesus commissioned his church to function as the light of the world and the salt of the earth. In the context of his teachings the meaning of these figures of speech is clear: The church is to bear the message of the good news of the gospel to all people everywhere.

There was a time when this was comparatively simple. One merely shared the message of God's love and grace with one's family, neighbors, friends, and associates. Now, however, our world has suddenly changed. Our circle of daily contacts has become radically larger and far more complex. Though simple one on one witnessing is still important—and always will be—it is not enough.

It is not enough for three reasons. First, because of the way in which the world's population is so rapidly increasing, it is impossible for the church to keep pace with this growth by merely making individual contacts by word of mouth. Unless the church begins to change its methodology it will not be able to fulfill the Lord's great commission.

Second, the technological advances of the last few years have put new tools at our fingertips that can enable the church to reach multitudes rather than people individually. Relatively few churches will be able to afford many of these tools, but there is one that is within reach of all—the computer. Many churches have already become computerized. Many others will be shortly. The computer is an instrument that can assist the church in its effort to accomplish efficiently and effectively the evangelization of the world.

Third, discoveries made in the area of the behavioral sciences, when applied to the mission of the church, will enable the church to reach people with an effectiveness never before thought possible. For example, during the last generation many insights were gained into the ways people are motivated. Likewise, at the opposite end of the behavioral spectrum, many discoveries have been made relating to what affects people negatively. For the church not to make use of this information would be not only counterproductive but foolish.

One group that has recognized the truth of this observation is known generally as "tele-vangelists." Whether nationally known or recognized only in their own communities through the use of local cable channels, these TV ministers have reached tremendous numbers of people. Whatever one's judgment may be regarding the value of these ministries, the fact is that their outreach has been quite effective.

These television evangelists, having captured their audiences visually, maintain a regular—usually monthly and sometimes more often—contact with them via direct mail. Statistics reveal that the amount of money received as a result of these postal solicitations is phenomenal.

Probably most of us would not want to emulate these well known personalities because of the excesses some of them have been shown to be guilty of. However, as the saying goes, we ought not to throw the baby out with the bath water. The fact that certain methods have been misused ought not to lead us to discard those methods. We should discard only their misuse.

By combining an overwhelming desire to fulfill the great commission with both the advent of certain technological advances and the motivational insights provided by the behavioral sciences, the church will be better able to fulfill its mission in this world.

One area in which the church is able to effect

just such a combination is direct mail. By a serendipitous prodding of the Spirit, which took place many years ago, I was led to experiment with the use of direct mail as a means of building the church. After over thirty years of experimentation with this medium, I am convinced that it represents a tremendous untapped resource available to the church.

I encourage you to use any or all of the ideas presented in this book. If you do, you will come to realize, as I have, that the use of direct mail will enable you to multiply the effectiveness of your ministry.

Needless to say, I am thankful to God for that nudge of the Spirit that led me to use this medium in a way that has brought glory to Christ and has helped to advance the cause of the church in this world.

My sincere thanks are also expressed to Lyle E. Schaller for the encouragement and help he has given me in the preparation of this book. Without him this book might not have been written.

Finally, I must express my thanks to the congregation of the Supplee Memorial Presbyterian Church (USA) of Maple Glen, Pennsylvania. Without the understanding and support of those many good people, my ideas would not have had an arena in which to be tried.

I

Why Direct Mail?

"It won't work!" This was the immediate response of Jim Stevens, one of the board members at First Church, to Pastor Johnson's suggestion that the church attempt to reach the community surrounding it by using a direct mail approach.

"I agree with Jim," Alan Edwards chimed in. "No one reads junk mail. There's just too much of it in our mail boxes every day."

"That's right! And besides, we can't afford to get involved in any outreach program right now," added Bill Peters. "Our attendance has been down, and that means income has been down, too."

The entire board of First Church agreed that something had to be done to stop the downward spiral they had been experiencing for several years, but they also agreed that a direct mail program was not it. Their meeting ended without any concrete plans being formulated.

Next month they would resume the discussion of the problem. Maybe they would come up with an idea.

It is amazing how many church leaders think like Jim, Alan, and Bill. "It won't work!" "No one reads junk mail." "It will cost too much."

The Effectiveness of Direct Mail

A little thought reveals the fallacy of the argument that direct mail won't work. The fact that our mail boxes are filled with "junk" mail each day should reveal that it *does* work. Companies are in business to make a profit and would not spend their precious advertising dollars in this way if it weren't productive. The fact is that direct mail does indeed work despite what may be the general attitude toward it. In fact, it is the thesis of this book that direct mail will give you the *most* results for the *least* time, effort, and money. This is not merely an opinion. It is a fact based on solid statistical studies.

A few years ago Robert Enstad wrote an article, syndicated by the Chicago Tribune Service, that spoke to this point. In it, Enstad indicates that while sales from direct mail marketing are growing at an estimated 15 percent each year, over-the-counter sales are increasing at a rate of only about 6 percent each year.

Another interesting fact cited by Enstad indicates that the Direct Mail Marketing Association (DMMA) has instituted several services for those who receive so-called junk mail. Since some people don't appreciate receiving all this unsolicited mail, the DMMA has provided a way for names to be deleted from mailing lists. They have also provided an opposite service for those who would like to have their names placed on more lists.

Enstad, quoting a representative of the DMMA, wrote: "We had about 80,000 requests from persons wanting to get on or off mailing lists. About 20,000 persons wanted less mail. 60,000 asked to receive more mail."

So much for the objection that no one reads junk mail! But what about the church? Will direct mail work when its purpose is to spread the faith of Jesus Christ, to evangelize? It will!

Is there proof? Certainly. Direct mail has been used by the church for evangelistic and other purposes since the first century. We should not forget that the books of the New Testament that are generally called "epistles" are really letters sent by Paul, Peter, and others to accomplish a variety of goals. In the book of Revelation, John *wrote* to the seven churches of Asia Minor.

Direct mail is not something new for the church. It is actually quite old. The only difference now is that due to the efficiency and generosity of the United States government, the church is able to use this medium with greater effectiveness and less cost than ever before.

The Most for the Least

Another fact should not be overlooked. It is not merely in the area of evangelism that the medium of direct mail may be utilized by the church. The ways the church may use the postal service to accomplish its goals are limited only by our imaginations. Direct mail is able to provide the most for the least in the areas of pastoral care, Christian nurture, stewardship, communication, and so on.

As this is being written I have been in the pastorate for thirty-five years. At the age of twenty, I became the pastor of a small congregation in north central New Jersey. If there was a crowd, we could count on thirteen or fourteen people in the pews on Sunday morning. The only reason the denominational officials were willing to allow an inexperienced and untried person like myself to serve as the pastor of that congregation was that the only alternative to sending me was to close the church. I am convinced that those who sent me believed that it was only a matter of time before I would leave and the church would be closed.

For some reason still unknown to me I began to use direct mail to reach out to the community. It had an immediate and dramatic effect. When I left that congregation seven and one-half years later, the church had grown considerably, and the sanctuary was usually filled to near capacity. During that period several building programs were completed and the sanctuary was redecorated. The church still maintains a strong witness in its community as it approaches its centennial anniversary. In fact, it has just recently completed building new and larger facilities.

The second church I served was in a totally different type of neighborhood and was considerably larger than the first. Despite the differences, the use of direct mail had a positive impact over the ten and one-half years I served that congregation, though not nearly so dramatic as in the first church.

I am now in my eighteenth year as pastor of the third congregation. From the beginning the use of direct mail has had a place of paramount importance. So much mail is sent that some of the members complain about the volume. These complaints have done nothing to make us change our attitude toward its use. Nor have they caused us to reduce the amount. We believe, as Lyle Schaller says, that "redundant communication" is an absolute necessity. As the following statistics will show, the results have been extremely gratifying.

21

On the first Sunday I preached as the pastor of the third church, 109 people attended the morning service. It should be kept in mind that on the first Sunday of a pastorate the congregation is usually larger than on subsequent Sundays since even many inactive members will show up to size up the new preacher. Sixteen years later, we were averaging between 350 and 375 in the two Sunday services. This represented approximately 60 percent of our membership of 600. We recently completed a $1,500,000 building program to accommodate the increasing attendance at all of our church activities.

During this same period, the church budget rose from $24,000 to almost $300,000 with approximately one-third of this designated for missions and benevolences. One benevolence project I have emphasized in each of the churches is the One Great Hour of Sharing Offering. The year before I accepted the call to my present church the congregation gave a total of $70 to this cause. One year later this amount was increased to slightly over $600. In my eighteenth year, the congregation gave over $15,000 in this offering.

Much of the growth experienced in my present church is due to the consistent use—some would say overuse—of direct mail.

So why use direct mail? Simply, because it

works! At this point we need to become personal as well as practical.

What will a consistent direct mail program do for your church? At least five things.

1. It will give both the pastor and the church a reputation for being progressive.
2. It will promote an image of an active church.
3. It will communicate a sense of strength and unity within the church.
4. It will call attention to and promote interest in the program of your church.
5. It will say to all on your mailing list that this is a church that is serious about its God-given responsibility to reach people for Christ.

Having made all of these positive statements regarding the value of direct mail to a local church, I do not want to leave you with the impression that the use of direct mail is a panacea. It will not in and of itself cure whatever may be ailing the local church. Also, it will not work by itself.

To grow a strong church a proper balance of six factors, of which direct mail is only one, is needed.

Preaching. A strong church will have a strong preacher whose message is biblically authoritative. "Thus saith the Lord" will be the emphasis of each carefully prepared sermon.

Pastoral concern. The congregation that knows that its pastor is concerned about each of its members will respond positively to that pastor.

Participation. Luther referred to this as "the priesthood of all believers." A pastor cannot do everything, but he or she should do everything to bring about the greatest possible participation from the members of the congregation. Total mobilization of the membership will probably never be achieved, but it should nevertheless be the goal.

Program. The church with the greatest possible number of activities for every age group is the church that will attract the people in its community.

Publication. This is direct mail. Publication is necessary to inform not only the church's membership but also the community at large of what is happening in the church.

Prayer. This is placed last not because it is least important but because it is most important. As Luther stated in his great hymn, "Did we in our own strength confide, our striving would be losing." We need to take advantage of the divine resources God so graciously makes available to us.

The church that takes care to keep these factors in proper balance cannot help but experience growth.

II

Getting Started

"We've got to do something! Attendance is still going down. Our offerings are dropping. We just aren't doing our job as a church. Maybe the pastor's idea about using direct mail isn't too crazy at that." Alan Edwards had been won over, at least partially, to Pastor Johnson's point of view.

"But we can't afford to get involved in some sophisticated program of direct mail. It will cost too much to buy all the equipment we'll need." This was the objection voiced by Bill Peters. It was seconded by most of the other members of First Church's board.

"We can't afford *not* to do something," responded Bob Williams. "We're caught in a vicious circle, and we've got to break out."

At this point, Pastor Johnson interrupted with what was probably the most significant comment in that discussion. "Bob's right. We can't afford not to do something. The point is, however, that we don't need all sorts of expensive equipment to initiate a direct mail program. We can start with what we have. We already have a bulk mail permit, so even that won't add to our expenses. The only added cost will be the additional paper and the postage."

Begin with What You Have

Pastor Johnson was right again. To begin a program of direct mail, a church may begin with what it has, even if that is only a typewriter and a duplicating machine.

I want to share with you my personal experience of beginning a direct mail program in my first church. As you may recall, that church had a Sunday morning attendance of thirteen or fourteen.

We began with nothing more than a used Royal typewriter and a no-name brand mimeograph machine. This duplicator was one of the "no frills" type, nothing more than an open drum on a tray. It was hand cranked, and the paper was hand fed into it.

The "we" I mentioned was my wife and myself. Janet cut the stencils, and I did the writing and duplicating. Together we collated, stapled, addressed, and stamped. Our mailing list wasn't large enough to make it possible for us to purchase a bulk mail permit.

Our first attempt at direct mail outreach was an amateurish, eight-page, monthly newsletter. Publication of this continued throughout the almost eight years I remained as pastor of that church. During those eight years, however, the newsletter became a rather sophisticated—at least according to my standards at the time—piece of local church literature. It certainly accomplished its purpose as the main medium of communication from little St. Luke's Church.

The point is that you must begin somewhere, and that somewhere is where you are and with what you have. We discovered that once we started our efforts began to bear fruit. At first this fruit was of an unexpected sort.

The first few issues of *The St. Luke's Evangel* appeared with covers produced on the old wax mimeograph stencils that had been cut with a stylus. We graduated from this to a picture of the church reproduced by means of the then relatively new process of using an electronic stencil. This attempt at improvement caught the eye of a regular visitor to our church, who managed the printing plant for a large corporation. Though he was impressed by our attempt, he wasn't impressed with the finished product. Following the service one Sunday morning, he came to me with an offer. "If the church provides the paper, I'll go in to work early some morning and print the covers." Our newsletter put on a new face.

Several young people who had begun to attend St. Luke's Church under my ministry offered to help with the collation, stapling, addressing, and stamping. Each month we had a "party" around our kitchen table, preparing the newsletter for mailing. Others began to do some of the writing. A woman in the church typed the stencils. What had begun as the work of the pastor and his wife was now spread out over a larger group of volunteers. Janet and I were no longer working until 2:00 A.M. Most important, St. Luke's Church was beginning to grow.

What a church needs to begin a direct mail program may be broken down into five categories: hardware, supplies, personnel, finances, and a mailing list.

Hardware

Only two pieces of equipment fall into the category of being absolutely essential—the typewriter and the duplicating machine. Most churches already own this equipment.

A few suggestions should be made, however, regarding the type of equipment to buy when what you have needs to be replaced, or it becomes possible to purchase additional equipment.

It is a rule that your finished product, whether mimeographed or printed, will only be as good as your typewriter is able to produce. Therefore, you should have the best possible typewriter. A machine that has an interchangeable type element or daisy wheel and that is equipped with a carbon ribbon will produce the most legible copy. The ability to change type faces will allow for variety in the finished product.

Duplicating machines of the type usually found in churches, and described generically as "mimeograph" machines, fall into three categories: drum type, silk-screen type, and a combination drum–silk-screen type. The best reproduction is secured with the pure silk-screen type.

The possibility of upgrading to a photo-offset machine in place of the traditional mimeograph should be seriously considered. However, keep in mind that this is a true printing press and may intimidate some office help. Before purchasing such a machine, be certain that someone on your staff or a volunteer is both able and willing to use it.

You might also do well to consider the possibility of having all printing done by a local printer. With the advent of quick-printing shops, this is feasible and relatively inexpensive.

In addition to these absolute necessities, there are several pieces of equipment that fall into the category of being elective, but that are nice to have. If you opt for the mimeograph process, next in the line of importance is an electronic stencil maker. Many different brands are advertised and sold. Buy only that brand for which service is readily available in your area. At least one highly advertised brand cannot usually be serviced locally. Ordinarily it must be sent back to the factory for service. Since it may take weeks (months?) before the machine is returned, you will be seriously inconvenienced when service is necessary. Service, not price, should be the primary consideration when purchasing every piece of equipment.

An addressing system is also a nice addition to office equipment. In the beginning, something as simple as sheets of gummed labels may be used. However, as the mailing list grows, the inefficiency of this method will become evident. When thinking about the purchase of an addressing system, give serious consideration to a computer. Even a small computer, such as the Commodore 64—someone in your church may have one that is no longer being used—combined with a relatively inexpensive dot matrix printer is able to maintain adequately the mailing list of even a larger than average church. Using a simple database program, such as Timeworks "Data Manager," a single floppy disk will hold over 1,700 three-line addresses or 1,300 with four lines.

The advantages of a computer should be

evident. Not only will it maintain your mailing list in the most efficient and effective manner, but also it will enable you to produce many excellent pieces of mail using what is called "desktop publishing" software. The Macintosh computer has pioneered in this field and still has a slight edge over its competitors. However, software for the IBM and its compatibles is not far behind.

A word of warning: Before you buy any desktop publishing software, be certain that it is what you want and are able to use. Most of the software is quite expensive. What is not expensive usually has a number of characteristics that make it less than desirable. Investigate thoroughly before purchasing.

Another factor you may wish to consider in your evaluation of desktop publishing is the cost of the additional equipment required. To produce quality work you will need a laser printer that will print at least 300 dots per square inch. Anything less will produce results that give a ragged appearance. Also, when you purchase software for desktop publishing, be certain that it will "drive" the particular printer you own or expect to purchase.

An alternative to purchasing a laser printer is to have a local company produce material from your disk on a linotronic typesetting machine, which will produce superb camera-ready copy at 2,450 dots per square inch. Your local computer store or printer should be able to put you in touch with someone in your area who uses a linotronic machine.

You should become familiar with the concept of desktop publishing since in several years it will be commonplace and should be well within the ability of even many smaller churches to purchase the necessary equipment. The November 1987 issue of *Changing Times* had an excellent article entitled "Desktop Publishing and Office Automation." It contains all the basic information you will need to evaluate desktop publishing and its application to your specific needs. The November 1987 issue of *Personal Computing* contains a lengthy guide to desktop publishing software.

Other pieces of equipment you may wish to consider are an electric stapler, a folding machine, a lettering machine and a simple collator.

If you have neither the equipment nor the funds to purchase it (see section on finances), do not allow this to stop you from initiating a direct mail program. Begin with what you have and do your best. As your program grows, you will discover ways to acquire new and better equipment.

Supplies

Regarding supplies, there are but three things to be said. First, buy in quantity. It is always cheaper to buy a case of duplicating paper than it is to buy a single ream. It is even cheaper to buy in ten-case lots. In some areas it may be feasible for a group of churches to form a co-op. If a paper dealer knows that a truckload of paper can be sold, the price will be unbelievably low.

Second, buy from discount suppliers. It is sometimes cheaper to purchase supplies from a discount dealer halfway across the country than it is to buy from the stationary store around the corner. However, do not buy on the basis of telephone solicitation unless you are certain that the offer is genuine and the dealer is reputable. Many scams have been perpetrated on unsuspecting churches in this way.

Companies that send out catalogs—such as the Quill Corporation in Northbrook, Illinois—are reputable and offer excellent prices. If you get on their mailing list, you will receive periodic sale catalogs that list even lower prices than the regular discount prices. Some of these companies offer free shipping if your order meets a prescribed minimum.

Third, look for "freebies." Large paper houses, for example, offer periodic closeouts. These are not usually advertised, but if you ask for a list of closeout items, you will find that it is sometimes possible to buy paper and envelopes at a small fraction of the original price.

This isn't really a "freebie." Some are available, however. If there is a printer in your congregation, ask about the possibility of securing "leftovers." It may just be that the printer will give you what cannot be used in order to obtain a tax write-off. You may get some odd sizes of paper, but design your direct mail pieces to fit the materials available.

Personnel

Using the services of young people has already been mentioned. At the other end of the age spectrum, don't forget those in your church who are retired. This is an area in which the services of senior citizens can be extremely helpful. Everyone who has avoided work with the excuse, "I don't have any talents the Lord can use," *can* fold paper, seal envelopes, and use a stapler.

Enlisting the aid of otherwise uncommitted members will accomplish more than merely getting your direct mail program started. It will give these people what they need to get them into the center of the life of the church.

Finances

It is false economy to try to save money by cutting back on direct mail outreach. Ask a member of any church that has tried this approach, and you will learn that it has always more than paid for itself. However, there are ways to finance the program and the purchase of equipment.

Put the direct mail program into the church budget. As the leaders of your church see what a direct mail program is able to accomplish, they will become increasingly willing to allocate funds for this purpose. Be prepared for resistance, but remember that "No!" really doesn't mean not at all.

Make your needs known through your newsletter and your Sunday morning church bulletin. It is amazing how many people will respond to announcements of this sort by making contributions to the purchase of a specific piece of equipment. It is equally amazing how many pieces of used, but otherwise good, equipment are donated to churches as a result of such announcements.

Watch the classified ads for used equipment that is being sold. On one occasion, I purchased three complete addressing systems in a single lot even though we needed only one. We kept the one that met our needs and sold the other two for as much as we had paid for the three. It is the old story of one person's junk being another person's treasure.

Consider selling ads in your monthly newsletter. These will more than likely bring in sufficient revenue to cover the cost of the publication with some funds left over for other purposes. One person should be put in charge of securing these ads, though he or she may work with several others. I have found that women will usually be better at this than men.

The Mailing List

Of tremendous importance to the direct mail program is the mailing list. It should be considered a rule of thumb that a church's mailing list should be twice as large as the number of families included in its membership. It should be even larger if possible.

You build your mailing list by beginning with the names and addresses of church members and by adding the names of all nonmembers who have an association with your church through the Sunday school, youth fellowship, women's association, nursery school, or any other organization your church sponsors.

Add to this basic list the names of visitors to your church. To secure these names and addresses, do not rely on a visitors' book in the narthex or on cards kept in the pews. The majority of people simply will not sign these. Instead, utilize what is called a "Ritual of Friendship." At a specific point in the service each Sunday morning, each person in attendance, members and visitors alike, is asked to give complete names and addresses on a form and to place a check in one of two columns to indicate whether he or she is a member or a nonmember. On Monday morning, the names and addresses of the visitors are noted and placed on the mailing list.

Anyone who shows even the slightest interest in the church should be placed on the mailing list. Send newsletters to all who are willing to receive your literature for as long as they are willing to receive it. The reason for this is expressed in the saying, "The church they know is where they'll go." If your church establishes a contact with an individual or a family and continues to maintain that contact, your church will be "their" church, even if they attend only at Christmas and Easter. The fact that you have even one or two opportunities each year to minister to these people could mean that at some point they will make a lasting commitment to Christ and your church.

III

Copy That Gets Results

"I still don't think we can put together a direct mail program that will work," Bill Peters said to his fellow board members after they had voted to try Pastor Johnson's suggestion. "We don't have anyone in our congregation with artistic or editorial ability."

"Don't be too sure about that," the pastor responded. "I've already contacted Lori Beth Wilson and Susan Johansen, and they've agreed to work on this project if I work with them and provide the ideas. Lori Beth majored in art in college, and Sue was the features' editor of her high school newspaper. Both of them have some experience in laying out the sort of things we want to do."

Ever the pessimist, Bill came back with another objection. "I don't want our church sending mail to my friends and neighbors that advertises the fact that we're a bunch of amateurs. What we produce ought to look professional."

First Church had a wise pastor who had done

his homework. "Look, Bill," Pastor Johnson responded. "It doesn't have to look like some Madison Avenue P.R. firm did it for us. It simply has to tell our story and be reasonably attractive. At that 'Direct Mail for Churches Seminar' I attended I learned that there are really only a few principles that need to be followed to produce copy that works. These principles are easy to apply, and the more we use them the more professional we'll get."

Wise indeed! Pastor Johnson had taken the time to secure some basic education in the field of direct mail and had digested what he had been taught.

Actually only two basic factors must be taken into consideration if you wish to produce copy that gets results: *eye appeal* and *content*.

If you wonder why eye appeal is placed before content, there is a reason. Ordinarily we would expect content to be given primary consideration since what churches deal in is the gospel. Our message, what we have to communicate—the content—is primary. The way we do it is secondary. This is true empirically. Practically, however, the people we are trying to reach may not have the slightest interest in the content of our message. If the "package" in which we place the gospel isn't attractive, they may never even get to the content. Therefore, the emphasis is on eye appeal before content.

Factors That Contribute to Eye Appeal

Composition

In the area of the arts, composition is the practice of combining the various elements used to produce a harmonious end product. It may also be described as a "visual symphony."

To achieve proper composition, a number of factors should be kept in mind.

a. Variety of Type Faces. The use of different type styles (though not too many and not radically different on a single page) will greatly enhance the appearance of the work you produce. Several products will allow you to produce materials using an almost unlimited combination of type faces.

The most obvious, of course, is your typewriter. If you have one that uses changeable typing elements, a change in typestyle within the text of the material is simple.

But what if you want to do headlines or have one section stand out from the rest of the text? You are still able to use your typewriter. Try using all caps, underlining, or set the typewriter for 10 pitch typing and use a 12 pitch typing element. Experimentation will produce many pleasing results.

However, if you want a headline that really

looks like a headline, you will need what is called "transfer type," which is available in most stationery and art supply stores under a variety of trade names. One of the brands that is most readily available is produced by the Chartpak Company. It comes in a vast number of styles and sizes. The advantages of transfer lettering are ease of use and low cost. The salesperson can usually explain its use, and practice can make virtually anyone quite proficient in its use.

b. Balance. The concept behind balance is exactly what the word implies. A well prepared piece of direct mail will have a balanced appearance. Balance may be achieved either symmetrically—everything is carefully measured—or optically—that which may not be symmetrical but which nevertheless looks balanced to the eye. As a rule, optical balance is the more effective of the two. Symmetrical balance is boring. Rather than go into great detail defending this point, let me call your attention to the illustrations on page 109, which should convince you. Those blocks marked "S" are illustrations of symmetrical balance, while those marked "O" show optical balance.

Optical balance is often described as what has been called "the rule of thirds." A page divided in thirds, either vertically or horizontally, will result in a design that is more attractive than one that has been divided into halves or quarters. Again see the illustrations on page 109.

c. White Space. White space refers to the margins as well as to the space between the typed copy and headings and/or illustrations. A layout with ample white space attracts attention because it is uncluttered and easy to read. Copy without sufficient white space discourages people from reading it.

Movement

Movement refers to the direction in which your copy causes the reader to move his or her eyes. In our Western culture the natural movement of the reader's eyes is from left to right and from top to bottom.

The layout of any piece of direct mail should allow the reader to move her or his eyes naturally over the copy. Helps for accomplishing this include arrows, dots, lines, a pointing finger, and so on.

Do not introduce anything into the copy that will interfere with this natural movement. For example, pictures of people within the printed matter should always be looking toward the text and not away from it. A picture near the left hand margin of a person looking to the left will lead the eyes away from the copy and thus distract the reader.

Justification of Copy

When lines of copy are "justified" the right hand margin will be even because all lines will be of equal length.

There is a difference of opinion regarding whether or not copy should be justified. However, any page in which columns are used should be justified. The narrower the columns the more important it is that the right margin be justified. Justified copy is more pleasing to the eye.

There are several ways to justify copy. Some typewriters and many computer word processing programs will automatically perform this function. However, it may be done manually, though it does require typing the material twice.

To justify manually, set the typewriter margins to the width of the line desired. Do not type beyond that width. If a line has *less* than the number of spaces required to fill it, complete the line with slash marks (/). When the typing has been completed go back over the copy. For every slash at the end of a line, place a pencil slash between words in that line. Spread the slash marks throughout the line so that they are not all together. Also, spread them in such a way that they do not occur directly under one another in succeeding lines if this is possible. Then, retype the copy, skipping two spaces between words rather than one wherever a pencilled slash mark has been placed. A good typist will learn this method of justification quickly.

An objection that has been raised to the use of justified copy is that the extra spaces between words are unsightly. This is not so since it isn't usually noticed by the reader. Take a daily newspaper and read any column, noting the spaces left between words to achieve justification. You see them when looking for them, but you have probably not been conscious of them before.

Illustrations

Aptly chosen illustrations always enhance the appearance of any piece of copy. Illustrations in the form of professional "clip art" may be purchased, or you may keep a file of those you have gathered from a variety of sources. Train yourself to look for good illustrations. When you find one, whether you have an immediate need for it or not, clip and file it for future use.

Don't think that you should always use illustrations with an obviously religious message. The message will be in the words that accompany the illustration.

Color

The use of color will add to both the attractiveness and the effectiveness of your direct mail pieces. Color adds life to your copy and helps to convey certain ideas that may be used to advantage.

Bear in mind the fact that color is symbolic. Think of the ways in which a variety of moods is introduced by color. We speak of *"red* letter days," *"rose* colored glasses," *"blue* Mondays," and so on. Color projects moods to the printed page.

Color may be introduced in several ways—by means of the paper, the ink, or both. Black ink on a colored sheet of paper may be quite effective. According to tests performed by the Direct Mail Advertising Association, the most legible copy is produced by means of black ink on yellow paper.

Use nothing but black ink for lengthy paragraphs since other colors create eye strain, which causes the reader to be psychologically "turned off" to the message you are trying to communicate.

Factors That Contribute to Good Content

Style

Style is the quality that gives distinctive character and excellence to artistic expression. Style is what makes people want to read what you have written. There is no need for the church to produce material that is as "dry as dust." Avoid what Herschell G. Lewis in an article in *Direct Marketing* magazine refers to as "The Bore/Snore Effect."

Jerry Huntsinger, the prince of direct mail for nonprofit organizations (he wrote the letters that raised the millions of dollars necessary to build Robert Schuller's Crystal Cathedral), suggests that to get results by direct mail one's style must be simple and homey. Use stories. Use short words (if possible 60 percent or more should be five letters or less). Use contractions. Emulate the style of publications such as *The Readers' Digest*.

Accuracy

Two forms of accuracy need to be noted. First is linguistic accuracy. Any piece of direct mail you send should exhibit accuracy in grammar, punctuation, and spelling without appearing pedantic. It is amazing how many people are literally offended by linguistic inaccuracies.

Second is accuracy of content. You should ask yourself the question, "Are the times, dates, names, precise locations, and the like given accurately?"

Completeness

When writing copy for publication, you should ask the question, "Have I told the whole story?" Journalism students are taught to include the five "Ws" in everything they write: who, what, when, where, and why.

Clarity

Every sentence should be crystal clear. Read and reread; then rewrite everything you write. Don't make statements that could be misunderstood or taken in two ways. What you write should be understandable to everyone who will read it.

Conciseness

Don't be wordy. Omit every word possible as long as the omission does not change the meaning of a sentence. Be a "word" surgeon. People don't want to wade through a mile of words if an inch is all that is needed.

General Rules

Don't promise more than you can produce. The tendency in much direct mail is to overdramatize the product to make it look better than it really is. If you do this in direct mail designed to advertise the church it will be immediately evident to your readers. People may accept this from secular advertisers but not from the church. The church should deal in truth.

You should learn to turn your liabilities into assets. If your church is small don't spend your time and effort bemoaning the fact that it isn't large. Capitalize on your size as it is and advertise your church as one that is "large enough to serve you well and small enough to want to." If your church is composed largely of older adults, advertise your specialty. Yours is "The Church with Senior Citizens in its Heart."

With a little effort, a bit of determination, and a willingness to apply the principles outlined in this chapter, you, too, will be able to produce copy that gets results.

IV

Direct Mail for Communication

"Since we started this direct mail program in our church, my mail box is always cluttered." Bill Peters was at it again.

Pastor Johnson felt personally attacked, but he remained calm and patiently responded to the complaint. "Bill," he said, "you can't deny the fact that the program has been working. Four new families have started coming to our church over the past few months as a direct result of our mail outreach."

"That's fine," Bill responded. "But those of us who are members don't need all the mail we've been getting. We know what's going on without it."

Alan Edwards chuckled. Unable to contain himself, he said good humoredly, "If you know everything that's going on at church, how come you missed the special board meeting we had last week? When I told your wife I had missed you she said that you didn't know about it. Pastor Johnson announced it last Sunday morning at the service. Wasn't that enough?"

"All right, all right. So I didn't hear the announcement. Maybe a postcard should have been sent to the elders, but I still don't think the entire congregation needs all the mail that's being sent," Bill remonstrated.

Bob Williams jumped into the conversation. "Bill, I think you just proved the fact that we do need mail to keep the congregation informed. I'm just like you. I remembered the board meeting, but Joan and I would have missed the young married couple's party if it hadn't been for the mailer we got about it. We heard the announcement in church but then forgot about it until that piece of mail came."

"It's what has been called 'redundant communication,' " Pastor Johnson said. "If we expect people to attend our programs, we've got to tell them about them over and over and in many different ways. The value of a piece of mail is that it comes right to your home."

Bill Peters wouldn't admit it, but he was in the process of being convinced of the value of the direct mail program First Church had instituted.

The Importance of Communication

The primary reason for a church to maintain a consistent direct mail program is communication, and the one great reason for communication, is to *inform*.

It is important to keep a congregation informed of all things that are happening. There are at least four reasons for this.

1. An informed congregation is an *involved* congregation.
2. An informed congregation is an *active* congregation.
3. An informed congregation is a *united* congregation.
4. An informed congregation is a *happy* congregation.

However, direct mail for communication is not merely aimed at the membership of the local congregation. It is equally important that nonmembers who have an interest in your church be kept informed.

The church they know is where they'll go. Some people attend church infrequently, maybe only once or twice a year. If your church keeps in touch with these people by mail, in spite of the fact that they are not members, your church will be "their" church. And, more important, when they do attend church, it will be your church they will attend. It is better to have an opportunity to be a witness to these people once or twice a year than not at all. Who knows, on one of those occasions Christ himself may put his hand on their shoulder and draw them to himself.

There is another reason for communicating with nonmembers via the mail. Often these people provide a link with others who are seeking a church. Many families have been introduced to one of the three churches I have served by those who weren't themselves members. These nonmembers knew about our programs because they were on our mailing list. When they were asked about churches in the community, ours was the one they recommended.

On special occasions you may wish to reach more people than are on your own mailing list. You may want to communicate with every home within a five- or ten-mile radius of your church to tell people about the dedication of your new educational wing or to invite them to attend your church's anniversary celebration. Under such circumstances, it is possible to buy mailing lists.

There are national organizations that sell such lists. The most convenient way for a church to locate a source of local lists is to consult the Yellow Pages under—what else?— "Mailing Lists." Even a rural or suburban area's phone book should list one or two sources for this service. If your phone book does not contain such a listing, consult the book for the nearest city.

Use direct mail to inform both members and nonmembers of your services, programs, and news about other members and special needs. In fact, any item of interest and importance to your church should be communicated by mail.

Forms of Communication

Direct mail may be used in a variety of ways as a means of communication. The most obvious form of communication is the letter. There are two categories of letters: personal and mass produced. Personal letters (though these also may be mass produced by computer and otherwise) will be considered in detail in chapter 7, "Direct Mail for Pastoral Care." We will, therefore, limit the discussion here to letters that can be mass produced and sent to the entire mailing list.

Only the imagination limits the number of applications of this form of direct mail. Letters may be used to advertise services, to make needs known, to recruit volunteers, to make financial appeals, and so on.

One letter that has worked well in my congregation is a pre-summer letter in which I set a goal for summer church attendance and encourage the congregation to help meet that goal. At the end of the summer, I send a follow-up letter, thanking the congregation for working hard to achieve the goal. My church has never failed to increase its summer attendance by this method.

We have also used the letter method to secure a "talent and interest profile" from each member. Properly written and prepared, letters produce excellent results.

Several general suggestions regarding the preparation of letters should be noted. When you write letters, remember the value of stories. People like to read about people. The human interest approach will usually capture the reader's interest better than any other.

As much attention should be paid to the format of the letter as to the content. It should *not* be written in the ordinary letter style. Some sentences, or even paragraphs, should be set apart by underlining or capitalization. However, be certain that what you underline or capitalize is what you really want to emphasize. To set apart an unimportant thought in this way is to call attention away from what is important. Headlines, line cuts, and other devices may also be used to dress up a letter.

Pay attention to the envelope. If you are going to use a plain envelope be certain it is exactly that—plain. No return address, no identifying logo or anything else that will reveal the sender should be used. Research has shown that the envelope without identification will usually receive priority attention from the recipient.

If a plain envelope is not to be used, use one with a "hook." A hook is nothing more than something that excites the readers' interest and makes them want to open the envelope to see what is inside. When one of my sons was carrying on a long distance courtship with the woman who is now his wife, he decorated the envelopes with all sorts of interesting, eye-catching illustrations. Not only did his wife-to-be want to get to the letter inside, but the postman did as well! At least that is what he told my daughter-in-law.

There are a variety of ways in which the plain white envelope may be decorated and thus transformed into a "baited hook." Volunteers, using brightly colored marking pens, may write messages across the bottom of each envelope, encouraging the potential readers to, "Open This First," or "Important Material Enclosed—Please Read in Full."

A rubber stamp may also be used to convey these messages. Remember, however, that the laws governing the use of bulk mailing permits require that each piece in a single mailing be identical. Of course, with first class mail this is not a problem. In fact, when using first class mail you may wish to add the name of the recipient. "Jean, Read This!" emblazoned in red across the front of an envelope is certain to get the attention of the recipient.

At this point a word should be said regarding the fact that a first-class postage stamp (commemorative, please!) serves as a hook. Studies reveal that the rate of response to first-class as compared to third-class mail is considerably larger. There may be times when your message is so important that it will warrant the extra expense of first-class postage. Remember, too, that third-class permit holders may use precancelled stamps that give the appearance of a first-class stamp.

Write long letters. Most people would react negatively to this suggestion, saying that long letters won't be read. Whether that is true or not is unknown. What is known is that long letters always produce better results than short ones whether or not they are read in full. Note the letters you receive from those who are trying to sell you something. They are usually four pages long.

Research has also shown that letters that contain a postscript produce greater results than those without one. The P.S. may be either typed in or, in some cases, handwritten. In situations where the letter contains an invitation to a special service or event, you may want to use the P.S. to say, "If you need a ride, call me at. . . . " Under other circumstances you may want to say, "If you want more information, my phone number is. . . . " By the way, one of the best ways to learn how to write a good letter is to study letters you receive from successful organizations.

Another form of direct mail churches could use for communication is the brochure. Like letters, brochures may be used for a number of different purposes and may have a variety of audiences in mind.

The postcard is often an overlooked form of communication. They may range from full color, professionally prepared photographs of your church to those that are produced on your church's mimeograph machine. Avoid the use of the pre-stamped government postcard, however. Studies show that this will not produce the results of other types.

Self-mailers have also been virtually unused by the church except for what have been referred to as newsletters. A self-mailer is usually a single sheet of folded paper (though it may be more) with the address placed on the advertising piece itself.

A self-mailer should *not* be secured with cellophane tape or a staple since a self-mailer should fall open easily. Staples are especially bad since the piece being mailed may be torn when it is opened, rendering at least a portion of it unreadable. This may leave a negative impression on the recipient. Worse yet is the possibility that the intended reader may prick his or her finger on the sharp points of the staple. It is usually best to use a somewhat heavier paper stock for the self-mailer since it will not have the protection of an envelope.

The communication "workhorse" for churches is the newsletter. For the church considering the publication of a newsletter, several preliminary questions should be posed.

How will it be financed? This will certainly be the major concern of your church board. If it is not contrary to the principles of your church, one of the best ways to finance the publication is through advertising.

How will it be printed? For a number of reasons a professionally printed newsletter is far more desirable than one that has been mimeo-graphed. Chief among these reasons is that the printed product has a more professional look about it and, therefore, leaves a much more positive impression on the reader.

The fact that it is professionally printed does not mean that it must be professionally typeset. Preparing camera ready copy in your church office is possible and even desirable. All that is needed is a good typewriter—the transfer type—and clip art—mentioned in a previous chapter—blue lined graph paper, and a glue stick.

What size sheet will be used? Church newsletters have been published in a variety of sizes: 8½" × 11" (unfolded with sheets stapled together); 8½" × 14" (folded once to 8½" × 7"); 11" × 17" (folded once to 8½" × 11"). The 11" × 17" format is suggested for several reasons. The first reason is a matter of economy. When you use this size sheet, it is possible for you to print two pages for very little more than the price of one 8½" × 11" sheet. Then, too, this is the size most people are accustomed to. Most school and business newsletters are printed in this size.

How many pages will it have? This may vary from month to month, depending on the number of articles contributed. However, under no circumstances should the number of pages exceed sixteen. Many people like to read the church newsletter in a single sitting, and more than sixteen pages makes this impossible for the average person. Twelve pages are ideal, according to a personal study I have made.

How often will it be published? It is probably most effective to produce a monthly newsletter, possibly skipping the months of July and August. If you elect to follow this schedule, mailings should be sent at other times during the month and certainly during the summer hiatus. Remember the need for redundant communication.

What personnel will be needed? The pastor may

need to assume almost total responsibility at first, but should enlist other help as soon as possible to do as much of the work as possible. It should be the pastor's goal to be totally relieved of the responsibility for this, except for writing the pastor's column, which should be a regular monthly feature. Ultimately, personnel needs will include the following: editor-in-chief, advertising editor, layout editor, writers, typists, and proofreaders. The functions and responsibilities of these people should be evident.

What should be included? Every major function of your church should be announced in the newsletter prior to the event's occurrence and should also be reported in the following issue. Every organization should have its own regular column (a suggestion: assign the length of all articles in number of words, since would-be authors often tend to be wordy).

Use names. Use as many names in each issue as possible, since people enjoy seeing their names in print. One way to assure that the name of every member and friend of your church will appear in the newsletter at least once each year is to publish a list of birthdays. These birthday announcements should appear one month in advance—that is, January birthdays should appear in the December issue. This allows people to purchase and send greeting cards to their friends. You see, this publication will encourage your members to begin their own personal direct mail programs.

Goals relating to the use of names should be set. First, each issue of the newsletter should carry the names of at least fifty people. In larger churches this number will, of course, need to be increased. Second, in smaller churches every person's name should appear in the newsletter at least three times each year; in middle-sized congregations (300-1,500), twice each year; and in churches over 1,500, once each year, though more often is preferred.

Larger churches may wish to use a newspaper format to accomplish what smaller churches do with the newsletter.

Some denominations (The United Methodist Church, for example) provide a newspaper service for their churches. A local church may contract with a denominational organization for this service. The church is responsible for providing material for one or two newspaper-size pages. The other pages contain news of general interest to the people of that denomination and are the same in the newspapers of all the churches that subscribe to the service. The main advantage of this arrangement is lower printing costs. Because of the volume of newspapers produced, the denomination's printer is able to produce the newspaper much more reasonably than can a local print shop. The major disadvantage is the limitation of space for local news, since, at most, only a few of the total number of pages are allocated for this purpose.

Churches that may want to devote the entire newspaper to local church news may consider a local printer. Most weekly newspapers are equipped and prepared to print a church newspaper.

It should also be remembered that postage for a newspaper may be more economical than for a newsletter, since postal regulations allow a newspaper to be mailed *within a county* at a special rate.

In designing direct mail for communication, use your imagination and go as far as it will take you.

V

Direct Mail for Evangelism

"The first suggestion I want to make in my new role as chairperson of the evangelism committee is that we approve a program of outreach by mail to the community within a five mile radius of our church."

The other members of the board of First Church couldn't believe what they had heard. Pastor Johnson's face broke into a broad smile. He knew it had been coming. Bill Peters had told him that he was going to bring up this topic. In fact, it was the reason Bill had asked to be made chairperson of the committee.

"Don't look so shocked," Bill said to his fellow board members. "I've been convinced. It's evident that what has been happening around here is a result of our direct mail program. Only a fool would deny that the mailings we've sent out have been successful. Look, a lot of thinking has gone into my decision, and I've got a full scale plan to present, if you people will stop looking so dumbfounded and if someone would just second my motion."

In the shock of the moment, the board had forgotten that motions were meant to be seconded. Mary Williams was the first to respond. "I second Bill's motion."

"Thanks, Mary. Now, let me get back to my idea," Bill said. "In thinking through this matter of outreach by mail, I believe that it would provide an ideal vehicle for what I think of as indirect evangelism. Some others, I believe, have referred to it as pre-evangelism. We can use the mail to get people's attention so that they'll give us a hearing. This is what I have in mind. . . . "

Bill was right. Direct evangelism usually needs more of a personal touch than you are able to achieve in a first-time contact with a family by mail. Such an approach could backfire and drive people away. However, an innovative direct mail outreach can influence people to come to church, where the gospel can be presented.

The Target Group

The first question to be considered when planning a direct mail outreach to the community is, "What is our target group?" Such an outreach program may be aimed at the public in general or at specific groups, such as women, men, young people, children, and newcomers to the community. Bill's idea, expressed in his motion, was an outreach aimed at the general public.

Once the target group has been determined, some other questions must be asked.

Sources of Names

For Bill and his committee, the most important question was, "If we want to reach everyone within a five-mile radius of the church, how do we get the names and addresses of these people?"

There are several possible responses to this. One is that you don't need the names and addresses. It is possible to send out mailings just as large companies do by simply addressing the piece of mail to "Occupant." This has been tried successfully by some churches. If this method is used, the words "To Our Friends At" or some other more personal designation should be substituted for the word "Occupant."

This, by the way, is an ideal way to reach people who live in those impregnable fortresses we call apartment complexes.

Since the more personal a piece of mail

appears to be, the more likely the recipient is to open it and read it, extra trouble should be taken to secure exact names and addresses. This, however, brings us back to that question of how to get these names and addresses. There are a variety of ways in which they may be gotten. Voting lists may be secured. Someone may spend a day at the county seat, copying the records available there. And, of course, a list may be purchased. The simplest means of securing the list is by what has been called a "reverse," or "criss-cross," directory. Several of these are published, but one of the most used is the one produced by Cole Publications, 901 Bond Street, Lincoln, Nebraska 68501.

A reverse, or criss-cross, directory is a telephone directory—or what some call a city directory. However, rather than being alphabetically arranged by the residents' names, it is arranged alphabetically by streets. Following the street and number is the name of the family living at that address.

With a city map, you determine the streets or portions of streets that are within the particular target area. Using the criss-cross directory, you can address the mail personally to each family.

One problem with such directories is their expense. It may be possible to borrow one from some large company. If the need is mentioned at a church board meeting, it is not unlikely that one of the members will have access to one.

The Envelope

Several suggestions should be considered regarding the envelope to be used.

1. Use a plain white envelope for the reason previously suggested.
2. Have volunteers hand address the envelopes, since this increases the probability that the piece of mail will be opened.
3. Use a pre-cancelled stamp rather than the nonprofit indicia usually used by holders of third-class permits. This gives the envelope the appearance of a piece of first-class mail and thus increases the probability that the envelope will be opened and the enclosure read.
4. Place the stamp on a slight angle. Studies have shown that this practice increases the probability that the mail will be opened and read. Why this works, no one knows. It just works!
5. Do not seal the envelope completely across the gummed edge. Studies reveal that envelopes that are difficult to open— and may cause a paper cut—tend to leave

a negative impression on the recipient. You want those who receive your mail to feel positive toward your church.

Timing

Since timing is of the utmost importance, another question that must be asked is, "When should the mailings be sent?" The answer to this question should be self-evident. Ask yourself another question: "When are people most likely to attend church?" Christmas and Easter. Thus the best time to do a community-wide mailing is prior to either one of these seasons. Remember: *The church they know is where they'll go.* An unchurched family, thinking of attending a church on one of the two major festivals of the Christian year, is quite likely to choose to attend your church because of the mail they have received. In fact, even if they aren't thinking of attending church, they may be prodded in that direction by your mail.

With regard to timing, one other factor should be given consideration. Tests performed by several direct mail organizations reveal that mail that arrives on Tuesday is usually most effective. There are several possible explanations for this. However, the explanations are not as important as the fact. Schedule your mail to arrive on Tuesday.

Another important question that should be addressed is, "Is one piece of mail sufficient to accomplish our purpose?" We respond to this by asking you to answer another question. Does a company that is trying to secure your business send you only one piece of mail? You know the answer. One piece of mail is not enough. My church has used a series of four mailings prior to Easter quite successfully. The first three mailings consist of what could be called flyers, while the fourth is an eight-page tabloid newspaper. They are mailed at two-week intervals, with the first to reach the recipients prior to the beginning of Lent and the last to be received just before the beginning of Holy Week.

Let it be said that the results of such a mail program are not all immediate. There is what might be called a residual effect. A number of interesting results were realized as much as four years after the mailings were sent.

Specific Groups

There are several specific groups of people who are important enough to warrant speaking specifically about direct mail programs aimed directly at them.

Reaching newcomers to the community is

always a challenge. A direct mail approach to this group provides an ideal solution to what has always been a problem.

The major question once again is, "How do we discover who the newcomers to our community are?" It is extremely difficult, particularly in urban areas, to locate and identify those who fall into this category. Admittedly it is difficult, but it is not impossible. Real estate agents have access to real estate transfer lists. These lists include the names and addresses of all new families who have purchased homes in your community. A real estate agent in your church or one who is a friend of your church could provide you with these lists when they are published. If you live in or near the county seat, a visit to the proper office could also provide you with the information you desire—and much sooner than the published lists. In some areas, local utilities will also supply churches with the names and addresses of those who have recently moved into the community.

Just recently a new service has been made available. The change of address cards that people send to their post office six or eight weeks before they move are now being sent directly to Washington, D.C. Several large companies are buying these lists and make them available at a cost of only pennies per address. Because of computerization, it is now possible (theoretically, at least) to have these names and addresses prior to the time the person or family has moved into their new home in your area. One of the companies from which you may purchase these lists is the Specialized Ministries Center, 855 Welsh Road, Maple Glen, Pennsylvania 19002.

To increase the effectiveness of your outreach by mail, use a series of mailings rather than just one. The series should consist of two letters and a copy of your most recent newsletter. All of these, of course, should be sent by first-class mail and should at least have the appearance of being personally written to the family or individual.

There are several ways to accomplish this individualization. In communities where newcomers are few, the letters may be individually typed by the church secretary and signed by the pastor. In larger communities, where the number of changes among homeowners may be several hundred each month, it would be impossible to type each letter individually except by computer.

Even without a computer, however, it is possible to individualize each letter. A sample letter should be typed on your church letterhead, using a typewriter equipped with a carbon ribbon. Leave sufficient space at the top of the letter for the date, the recipient's name and address, and the salutation. Sign the sample letter, using a fine to medium point felt tip pen. Have this letter reproduced by a printer, using the photo-offset process. Then, using the same typewriter with the same typing element, insert the specific date, name, address, and salutation. This will give the letter the appearance of having been individually typed.

The reason for the signature with the felt tip pen is that this, better than any other method (except, of course, actually signing each letter) gives the appearance of having been individually signed.

Include with your first letter a promotional piece that tells something about your church and its worship hours. Include some of this same information in the body of the second letter.

The two letters and the newsletter should be sent at one-week intervals. Also, the suggestions regarding the plain white envelope, the handwritten address, and the angled stamp should be observed. Since these will be sent by first-class mail, go to the extra trouble of using a commemorative stamp. This, too, will increase the possibility of the letters' being read. Samples of the two letters are included in the appendix.

Another specific group of people for whom a direct mail outreach has proven effective is visitors to your church. Their names and addresses are secured from the "Ritual of Friendship" pad mentioned in chapter 2. These people have sought you out and should, therefore, be given special attention.

On Monday morning, the first thing the church secretary—or better yet, a volunteer— should do is collect the "Ritual of Friendship" forms from the pews. The forms should be checked and the names and addresses typed on envelopes (this time bearing the name and address of the church). A form letter, prepared in the same way as those suggested for new residents, may be used. This letter from the pastor should thank the people for their visit and invite them to return.

Two different letters should be written. One should be prepared specifically for those who live in your community and the other for those who live at a distance from your church. The reasons for sending letters to those who live at a distance are that it is possible that the visiting person or family was in your town for the purpose of being interviewed for a position with a new company and may be relocating to your community. If this is the case, the letter is of the utmost importance. However, even if this is not the case this letter is important. The visitor may be a friend of, or related to, someone in your church or community. To make a positive impression on the visitor is to make a positive impression on that person's friend or relative.

A letter to a visitor from the pastor during the early part of the week after having attended your church should be only one of two approaches to that visitor during the first week. My church has established a corps of friendly volunteers who call on visitors within forty-eight hours of their first visit to the church. These visitors take a bud vase with a flower and a brochure describing the church. This never fails to make a positive impression on the family visited. They know that they have found a friendly church that cares.

Some churches try to reach visitors on the same day they first appear at worship. This may be by a phone call or a personal visit. Those who do this claim that the results are appreciably greater than if a call is made later in the week.

A third group that needs special attention is men. Men have consistently proved to be a most difficult group to reach. A direct mail approach may reach them when no other will.

The men's mailing list should be made up of those who have some sort of relationship with the church. They may be husbands, fathers of Sunday school children, and so on. This mailing list should include all men in any way related to your church whether they attend or not. It should be made clear in an initial letter to all on this list, and thereafter in a letter to all who are added to the list, that the letters are sent to *all* men who are related to your church. This will help to avoid the criticism that you are being judgmental by singling out certain non-church-going men for your evangelistic mailings.

With regard to format and content several facts should be noted. A standard logo should be used. (See the sample included in the appendix as an illustration of the type of logo you may use.) There should be good reason for everything that is included in the logo.

In the upper left hand corner, the place to which the eye goes first, there is a camera shutter with the word *Focus* in large letters. In smaller letters are the words, *getting your life in. . . .* This is meant to appeal to a universal need. No one, no matter how well adjusted, doesn't have some area of life that is "out of focus." The unspoken promise is that this letter will help clear up those problem areas in one's life.

Note also the words, *Written for men who are willing to think.* The words appear in the midst of a large expanse of white space in order to call attention to them. The implication of these words is that if you do not read the letter, you are unwilling to think. Only an idiot would be willing to make this admission, and not many are willing to place themselves in this category!

The layout of the letters is also important.

Portions should be centered, others staggered, some underlined. This is done for the purpose of emphasis.

When preparing a letter, you should try a variety of layouts until just the right one has been achieved. The "right" one is the one that places the emphasis in just the right places.

The content is of extreme importance. If you indicate, for example, that the letter was "written for men who are willing to think," the content should challenge the reader to use his gray matter.

Many other forms of direct mail ministry are possible. You may wish to reach out evangelistically to those who have had special experiences, both happy and sad. For example, births, weddings, and deaths are a matter of public record and are often noted in local newspapers. A short note or some other acknowledgment of one's special experience may provide just the nudge necessary to bring that person to Christ and the church.

Direct mail may also be used to start new groups and classes, to promote attendance at Christmas Eve, Easter, and Homecoming Sunday services and to build interest in your Sunday school for both children and adults.

Once again it may be noted that in the area of evangelism, the variety of ways direct mail may be used is limited only by your imagination.

VI

Direct Mail for
Christian Nurture

"I wonder if there is some way we can use direct mail to help deepen our members' commitment to Christ and the church?" Mary Williams was thinking out loud as she expressed this sentiment to the Christian Nurture Committee of First Church. She had chaired this committee for two years, and the committee never seemed to do anything that really affected the lives of the congregation in a positive way. She had seen how the introduction of a direct mail program had worked in other areas of the church's life and believed that there must be some way to use this tool to help people grow in their Christian faith.

"You know, I'll bet that if we spent some time thinking about it we could come up with at least a dozen good ideas," Mark Thompson responded. "Why don't we take thirty or forty-five minutes right now to do some brainstorming?"

They did, and they did—that is, they took

some time to discuss the subject, and they came up with a number of workable ideas. This was another illustration of the fact that the only limiting factor was their corporate imagination.

When a business employs direct mail techniques it is usually for one purpose—to attract customers to buy that business' goods or services. The church may use Direct Mail for Christian Nurture a similar purpose—to attract people to its services.

However, because the church is the church, its purpose in using direct mail should go beyond merely "attracting customers." One of the reasons for the existence of the church is to provide spiritual nurture for its members. This should, therefore, be one of the purposes in the church's use of direct mail and direct mail techniques. As has already been noted, Paul and others used letters to help people grow in God's grace and in their faith. And so should we!

Materials suitable for this purpose may be secured from several sources. Many commercial publishers produce materials designed to encourage Christian growth. For example, the devotional booklet *The Upper Room* may be purchased in quantity and sent, with a cover letter encouraging its use, to everyone on the church's mailing list.

In my opinion, however, this is merely second best. The best approach is to design and produce your own "home grown" materials, since they are certain to be more personal and, therefore, more likely to be used.

Capitalizing on Various Factors

When preparing such material the one word to keep in mind is *capitalize*.

Capitalize on the seasons of the church year to encourage the members of your congregation to become involved in an exercise of spiritual nurture. During Advent and Lent, for example, people's minds are naturally focused on spiritual subjects. Use this natural predisposition of the mind to encourage spiritual growth.

Even if yours is a church in which the terms *Advent* and *Lent* might be objectionable to some, use the concept if not the terms. Speak of the pre-Christmas and pre-Easter seasons.

Capitalize on the psychology of numbers. If the congregation as a whole becomes involved in a spiritual exercise, people who might not participate on an individual basis are likely to be pulled along by the crowd. All peer pressure need not be negative.

Capitalize on the abilities and the spiritual gifts of your church members. Have them write and sign the materials that are to be used. This will accomplish Christian nurture in two ways.

First, it will cause those who accept this responsibility to gain the benefit of thinking through the subject on which they are writing, which is Christian nurture in its own right. Second, it will cause others to read the materials, since they will want to know what their fellow church members have written.

I have personally used this approach on a number of occasions. In the fall we begin preparation for the Lenten season of the next year. One year we divided the Gospel of Mark into forty-seven sections, one for each day of Lent, including Sundays. I then contacted forty-seven members of the church and asked each of them to write a devotional article based on one of these passages. They were given the following explicit instructions:

1. Write an article consisting of *no more* than 250-300 words.
2. *Do not* try to be scholarly. Tell, in your own way, what this passage means to you.
3. Prepare a short, fifty word prayer that relates to and has grown out of the article.

In addition, a deadline was given, and each person was told that the material prepared would be subject to editing, though editorial changes would be kept to a minimum in order to maintain individual style.

When all of the articles had been received

they were edited, typed, and bound together into a fifty-two-page booklet, including a title page, an introduction by the pastor, and the forty-seven devotional articles. The back page was left blank. The title given to the booklet was *The Ministry of the Master*, which was based, of course, on the theme of Mark's Gospel.

The title page contained not only the title but also the subtitle "A Series of Lenten Devotions Based on the Gospel of Mark" and the statement, "By the congregation of . . . " followed by the name and address of the church.

Another year the same was done with the Gospel of Luke, and a booklet was produced under the title, *The Son of Man and the Sons of Men*. Again, the title was derived directly from the theme of Luke's Gospel. In each of these booklets the names of the authors and their vocations were published immediately following each article.

As a result of this personalized approach, practically everyone participated in the devotional reading of scripture during those Lenten seasons. The only problem encountered with this project was that many members of the congregation reported back to me that they had read straight through the booklet immediately upon receiving it because they wanted to see what their friends and fellow church members had written. However, most also told me that they also did the readings day by day so that the purpose was accomplished.

In another year, I challenged the congregation to "make Lent a time of feasting rather than fasting." The idea, of course, was "feasting" on the Word of God. The theme of the season was captured in another slogan—"Read the New Testament Through in Lent of '82." A Bible reading chart, a cover letter explaining the program, and a Bible Reading Pledge Card were sent to each member and friend of the congregation.

On the basis of the pledge cards received and the follow-up conducted after the Lenten season, it was determined that better than one-third of the congregation completed the reading of the entire New Testament during that seven-week period.

One of the attendant results of such Bible reading programs is that many who begin reading scripture as the result of a congregation-wide challenge continue reading it on their own when the group program has been concluded. Many even become involved in Bible study groups, since their appetites have been whetted through their reading.

It is also possible to coordinate such devotional materials with Sunday morning and Sunday evening sermons and even midweek Bible studies during these special periods of the church year.

Such a Lenten challenge could be based on the theme "The Will of God." The theme text would be Jesus' prayer in Gethsemane, "Not my will, but thine be done" (Luke 22:42). A series of sermons on the various aspects of

81

God's will could be prepared for Sunday mornings and evenings. Midweek services could feature messages by laypeople, relating to their personal experiences with God's will. A list of forty-seven Bible readings on the subject, a cover letter issuing a challenge to take God's will as seriously as Jesus did, and a brochure listing the various services and sermon subjects should be sent to the entire church mailing list several weeks prior to the beginning of the Lenten season.

"Life's Most Crucial Questions," "The Defeat of Death," and numerous other themes could serve as the basis for other coordinated Lenten services and devotional materials.

Pastoral Letters

In addition to full-scale seasonal programs, give consideration to using occasional letters whose specific purpose is to promote spiritual growth.

Again, the seasons of the church year should be seen as a reason for sending such letters. Use Advent, Christmas, Epiphany, Lent, Easter, and Pentecost to the best advantage by sending each member of your congregation a letter of challenge, inspiration, or encouragement.

Another reason for sending such occasional letters may be found in a special need within a particular church. For example, letters provide an excellent medium to communicate the principles of church growth to a congregation. Because of the limited amount of preaching time the average congregation is rarely introduced to subjects that are of great importance. They should be! Once again, direct mail provides the solution to the problem. The wise pastor is able to distill his or her knowledge of a given subject, put it into an easily digestible form, and pass it on to the flock in the form of a series of letters.

A good time for sending such a special series of letters is during the summer. At this season of the year the church is sending much less mail than at other times. It is good to take advantage of this summer slump to keep the church in the center of the congregation's thinking. Then, too, it is the time of year when most people have more leisure time and are more likely to give attention to their mail.

Another possibility is a regular pastoral letter. An interesting logo and a catchy title for this monthly publication (sent between issues of the newsletter) will help capture the readers' attention.

Do not use these letters to ask for money. Their only purpose should be for Christian nurture. To include a financial appeal is to confirm the sentiment expressed by so many that "The church is always asking for money." If a person's attention is distracted by the appeal for funds, the more important purpose of the letter will be overlooked and forgotten.

83

Do not use these letters to advertise your services. To include an announcement of a service in one of these letters is to encourage the reader to lose the message of the letter in the "commercial." The only exception to this rule is when the service is integrally related to the subject of the letter. It is far better to send two pieces of mail than to risk losing the reader's attention.

All of the discussion thus far has related to that mail whose primary purpose is to promote Christian nurture. Some mail may have Christian nurture as its secondary purpose. Included in this category are announcements of all special services, seminars, workshops, Bible study classes, Christian education electives in the Sunday school, and the like. Each of these programs has spiritual growth as its primary purpose. Therefore, mail that encourages attendance at these programs has spiritual nurture as its secondary purpose.

Preparation Guidelines

There are several rules to follow in preparing such announcements.

Use your imagination. Do not use dry-as-dust approaches. They will not attract people and will encourage them to believe that the program will be as dry as the material advertising it.

Much of the material in this book is taken from a seminar I conduct entitled "Direct Mail for Churches." I once made the mistake of allowing the director of an organization that was to sponsor a seminar to handle the publicity. He sent out a letter that, in terms of both format and content, violated all the rules that have already been stated. His material was of the "dry-as-dust" variety. The result was that the seminar had to be cancelled—no one, absolutely no one, enrolled.

Whenever we promote a seminar, we appeal to a need felt in virtually every church—the need to grow. Our mailings show a church bulging and bursting at the seams with people, some of whom are hanging out of the windows and doors. Accompanying this is the slogan, "YOUR CHURCH *CAN* GROW!" That approach gets results.

If your attempts at direct mail haven't produced results, you have probably been less than imaginative in your approach.

Be innovative. Don't be afraid to use new techniques. Search for ideas in the mail you receive from commercial organizations and tailor them to the needs of your particular church.

For example, why not buy some envelopes with a glassine window on the left side and design a series of mailings using some of the "hooks" that were mentioned previously?

If you want your membership to become involved in a discussion group, attach a shiny penny on the letterhead in such a position that when folded the coin will appear in the center of the window. Around the coin, place the words of the familiar saying, "A penny for your thoughts." It is guaranteed that not many pieces of that mailing will be thrown into the circular file. It may be "only" a penny, but virtually everyone will take the time to remove it from the letter and pocket it. Such an innovative approach will likely cause even the person who feels cool toward the church to at least glance at the contents of that letter.

The beauty of this particular method is that for only one penny more per piece you greatly multiply the possibility that your letter will be read. A little thought will produce many similar ideas.

Don't be afraid to challenge people to respond to a dare. It is a fact that the so-called "high demand" churches get a greater response from their congregations than those that make few, if any, demands. If you ask for nothing, you will surely get it.

If you elect to challenge your congregation to engage in a spiritual discipline, why not use the theme, "I Dare You?" Those words could be printed on both the envelope and the enclosed letter. Most people find it difficult to turn their backs on a dare.

Review the rules set down in chapter 3, "Copy That Gets Results."

VII

Direct Mail for Pastoral Care

"Pastor, I want to thank you for the letter you sent my wife last week when you heard that her mother had died. That letter meant a lot to her and to all of our family. It's nice to know that people are thinking about you when someone you love has been taken from you."

Several members of First Church's board were speaking informally following a meeting when John Marshall addressed this remark to Pastor Johnson.

Before the pastor could respond to John's statement, Alan Edwards said, "Pastor, it seems to me that you've been doing a lot of writing lately. Several people have remarked to me about the letters they've received from you. They've really appreciated them. What's happened?"

"Well," the pastor responded, "if you have a few minutes, and you really want an answer to your question, I have what I think is an interesting story to tell. You know Blanche

Norris. Well, I made a pastoral call on her several months ago. While I was sitting in her living room she all of a sudden said 'Pastor, I have something I've been wanting to show you.' She got up and went as fast as her eighty-five-year-old legs would carry her and got her purse. She sat down next to me, opened her pocketbook, and pulled out a discolored letter she had been carrying with her for years. She told me its story. It was a note from her former pastor, thanking her for some service she had performed for the church. That letter means so much to Blanche that she has carried it with her for who knows how many years. That experience got me thinking. I remembered the letters I had saved over the years. They weren't earthshaking, but they had special meaning to me. Then I thought that maybe sending short notes to people at special times in their lives would help to build a spirit of community in our church. So I determined to begin a letter writing ministry as part of our new direct mail outreach approach."

At that point, Pastor Johnson may not have even thought about giving a formal title to what he was doing, but he was actually using direct mail for pastoral care.

A pastor should anticipate three problems when initiating a letter writing ministry. First, this sort of ministry takes a tremendous amount of time. Second, do not begin it unless you are determined to continue it. If you send one person a letter and do not send one to another in a similar situation, you are inviting criticism. Third, recognize that even if you have the best of intentions there will be some situations in which you will err.

The Advantages of Pastoral Care by Mail

In spite of the potential problems, those who have used direct mail for pastoral care will tell you that the advantages to carrying out such a ministry far outweigh the disadvantages. Such a program does take a tremendous amount of time, but writing a letter takes far less time than making a pastoral call either in person or by telephone. Lyle Schaller, in the May 1980 issue of *The Parish Paper*, states that "Many ministers have discovered they can write two dozen notes in much less time than is required to *complete* twenty telephone calls or to make five home visits."

Another advantage of a letter over a telephone call or even a personal call to the home is illustrated by Blanche Norris (who, by the way, is a real person, though this is not her real name) and the way she cherished the letter from her former pastor.

Direct Mail Ministry

Blanche Norris is not alone. Just recently in a conversation with a woman in a retirement community, I was told of a letter she had kept in her Bible over a period of fifty-eight years. In 1928, when she became engaged, a former Sunday school teacher heard of the happy event and sent a congratulatory note. It meant so much to this woman that it was read, saved, and reread many more times throughout the years. It was also talked about. (A copy of this precious letter is now in my files.) A letter may be saved—and often is—while a telephone message or a visit to the home is soon forgotten.

There is also a psychological factor that should be remembered. Everyone likes to receive mail. Do you remember the statistic cited in chapter 1? When people had the choice of being deleted from or added to so-called junk mail lists, 60,000 chose to be added, while only 20,000 asked that their names be dropped. And here we are not speaking about junk mail but first-class mail.

Whether the person is a child accompanying his or her parent to the mailbox, a teenager longing for friendship, or a senior citizen who lives alone, everyone enjoys receiving mail. "What will the mail bring today?" is a question literally millions of Americans ask with the coming of each new day. There are more lonely people in your community than you would ever imagine. I am not a lonely person, but as I sit here writing this and look back over the events of the last eight hours I realize that today's high point for me was a piece of mail I received.

It takes little imagination to appreciate the joy that comes to a child of five or six years old when receiving a letter from her or his pastor on that child's first day of school.

It may take slightly more imagination—but only slightly more—to understand the joy a proud mother and father feel when this milestone in their child's life is recognized and acknowledged by the pastor. Such a letter could also be sent to those beginning high school or college. It is impossible to gauge the amount of good will this type of letter may create.

Methodology

Though this approach to pastoral care may seem to require an inordinate amount of time, several methods may be employed in this form of ministry to enable the average pastor to become involved in it without neglecting other areas of responsibility.

What is true of every other area of ministry is also true of this. One sure way to save time is to anticipate needs. *Plan!*

It is important, for example, to anticipate situations in which personal letters should be sent. The list should include birthdays, anniversaries, births, baptisms, deaths, welcome to new members, congratulations on special accomplishments, graduation, a new job, a job promotion, being mentioned in the newspaper, a financial contribution, participation in a church service, some special service to the church, years of faithful service, and the like.

To make the task of generating these letters even easier, these special occasions may be filed in the church's membership database by date so that a printout of the names and addresses of each day's recipients can be easily obtained.

Several of the occasions mentioned above deserve special comment. When sending a congratulatory note to someone who has been mentioned in the newspaper, include the clipping with the letter. This indicates to the person that he or she and his or her accomplishment have indeed been noticed.

A good ministry for someone who is elderly and/or shut-in is clipping articles from the local newspaper that relate to church members. These are then given to the pastor, who prepares the letters to be sent with the clippings.

"Thank you" letters should receive far more attention in the church than they usually do. Indeed, it might well be said that we have lost the fine art of saying, "Thank you." A common complaint against the church is that the church is always asking for something. And it is! However, that complaint would be voiced far less often if we practiced the grace of saying "Thank you" when someone has responded in a positive way to one of those requests.

Once you have anticipated the specific situations for which letters will be necessary, a logical next step is to anticipate the content of those letters. I recommend that they be pre-written; basic letters may be prepared in advance and modified to fit specific situations.

A computer becomes a tremendous asset at this point. Pre-written letters may be saved to a disk, called up on the screen, edited to fit a specific situation, and then printed on the church letterhead *using a letter quality printer*.

Several objections may be raised against this. Some would say that handwritten letters are far more effective than those that have been typewritten. This is probably true, but writing letters by hand takes far more time, and those whose penmanship is as poor as mine would do better to use a typewriter. I gave up sending handwritten notes when my oldest son, while in his first year of college, pleaded with me either to type my letters or stop writing to him.

Another objection that has been raised against computerizing letters is that it is cold and impersonal and represents an attempt to fool people into thinking they are receiving a personal letter when in reality they aren't. Is it better to send these letters, even if they are computer generated, than not to send them at all? The answer seems evident. Computer letters may indicate not an attempt to fool people, but an attempt to show concern for them. In a church with a membership greater than 200 it is almost impossible for one pastor to do everything required. To add a letter writing ministry to the pastor's other duties seems unreasonable.

If you or your church do not have a computer, this discussion has been purely academic. However, since more churches are computerizing, this approach to a letter writing ministry is both feasible and reasonable.

I would like to repeat a plea made in a previous chapter. Even a small computer is better than none. A Commodore 64, for example, is ideal for a small church. A request in your church bulletin or monthly newsletter may well reveal the existence of one that is not being used in the home of a church member. For a small investment in software you will be able to perform many tasks that are currently being done manually—but in a fraction of the time now required.

With a computer, it is possible to keep track of those special events in the lives of individuals even in a congregation of several thousands of people. The computer also enables the church secretary to merge this list with the proper pre-written letters with comparative ease. The pastor's only responsibility then is to sign each letter.

It should be unnecessary to say—but from personal experience I know that it needs to be said—that the pastor's signature should not be rubber-stamped. It should be personally signed. A rubber-stamped signature communicates a lack of concern and negates the value of the letter. It takes only a relatively short time to sign even several dozen letters. It is time well spent.

Several general suggestions need to be made regarding the preparation of the letters that have pastoral care as their purpose.

First, these letters should be from the pastor and not from the church. Therefore, they should be sent out on his or her personal letterhead and in an envelope with the pastor's name and address in the upper left-hand corner.

Second, use a commemorative stamp. Exercise care in the selection of that stamp, since many attractive stamps are available for this purpose. The use of a commemorative, rather than the usual first-class, postage stamp indicates that a little more care and concern went into the preparation of the message enclosed.

Third, though it has been said before, use only a letter quality printer in the preparation of these letters. A letter printed on a dot matrix printer shouts "Computer generated" to the recipient even if it was individually typed. This, of course, causes it to lose all of its value.

Give some thought to how much more you, as a pastor, will be able to accomplish if you undertake a ministry of pastoral care by mail. Give some thought also to the numerous ways in which this approach to ministry may be applied to your specific congregation. Even a little time spent thinking through the benefits and implications of a pastoral care ministry by mail should move you in that direction.

VIII

Direct Mail for Stewardship

"One of the things I don't understand is why the dramatic increase in membership and church attendance isn't reflected in our giving." Jim Stevens made this remark to the small group he was in charge of at First Church's annual leaders' retreat. All of the others in his group agreed that the increase in attendance hadn't made the sort of impact on finances that they had expected it would.

"Come to think of it," Alan Edwards added, "the increased attendance hasn't really made much of a difference in anything except the Sunday morning church services. The same old group of people is still doing all the work. Oh, there are some new members on our boards and committees, but for the most part, the same people do everything."

When Jim's group shared their insight with the others at the retreat, virtually all nodded in agreement. The consensus of opinion was expressed by Alan Edwards, who said, "The direct mail program certainly hasn't worked in the area of stewardship."

"That's not fair!" rejoined Bill Peters. In spite of the fact that virtually everyone at the retreat was solidly behind the direct mail program, now that Bill had been won over and saw its value, he felt personally attacked when someone questioned it. Bill's defensive attitude was evident in his tone of voice. "That's not fair! After all, we haven't really tried using direct mail to increase the stewardship response of our membership."

The rest of the group took his rejoinder good naturedly and even quipped about how "converts" to a cause are always the most fanatical.

Bill's defensiveness was defused by the jovial response, but he was not about to be put off. "Well, it's true," he said. "We haven't tried it, and we should. These new people don't really know anything about how much it costs to run a church, and they never will unless we tell them. Maybe they think they'll be intruding if they try to get involved. Maybe they think there's an old guard at First Church who don't want to be disturbed. What better way do we have to tell them about our financial needs and to invite them to become involved than by direct mail?"

Bill had indeed become a fanatical convert. But he was right. There is no better way.

Basic Rules for Stewardship Campaigns

Before getting to the specific details relating to direct mail and stewardship, several basic rules relating to all stewardship campaigns should be noted.

Be biblical. Stewardship and finances should not be confused. Stewardship involves finances, but it is much more. Stewardship, especially in the biblical sense, is related to ownership. Scripture teaches that God owns everything. What we say is ours really isn't ours at all; it is God's. God owns our "possessions." The Lord has simply given them to us to manage. In fact, scripture teaches that God owns us. This fact has many implications, but most important is the fact that this takes stewardship out of the realm of mere money. If God owns us, then we are responsible to God not only for the way we use our money, but also for the way we use our time and our talents.

Be tactful. A "soft sell" is always the best approach to teaching stewardship, especially in the area of money. There may be times when a "hard sell" is necessary; however, use it only when absolutely necessary. Do not make every need sound like an emergency. If you do, when there is a real emergency people won't believe you; remember the story of the boy who cried wolf.

Be goal oriented. Let the people of the church know what your goal is and continually inform them of how close you are to achieving it. In his book *Parish Planning*, Lyle Schaller says that, "In too many congregations too little is asked of the members—and the response is in proportion to the challenge."

One word of warning needs to be sounded at this point: Any goal that is set should be both challenging and realistic. Set it high enough to make people stretch, but not so high that it is impossible to reach.

Be complete. Tell the whole story. If you need money, state exactly how much is needed and why. If you need volunteers, indicate how many are needed and what they will be expected to do. It is also a good idea in some situations to tell the congregation what the consequences will be if the money is not raised or the volunteers do not come forward. However, use this negative approach sparingly. Save it for those previously mentioned emergencies.

Be optimistic. Indicate by your attitude and by the way you communicate with your membership that you believe in *both* the goodness of God and the generosity of God's people. An optimistic approach will always produce the greatest results.

Be enthusiastic. For some reason, Christians have decided that it is wrong to introduce enthusiasm into the church. "It isn't dignified," seems to be the prevailing attitude. Well, it is possible to dignify the church to death. Do you realize that the literal meaning of the word *enthusiasm* is "filled with God"? If Christians can't be enthusiastic about God and the church, then there is a deficiency in their faith.

Don't misunderstand. I am not speaking about unbridled enthusiasm. It is possible to be both enthusiastic and dignified.

The Specifics of Stewardship Appeals

Now, on to the specifics. Since so much has been made of the fact that stewardship is much more than finances, we should begin with a consideration of the way direct mail may be used to make people conscious of this fact and how it may also be used to encourage them to give of their time and special gifts as well.

One year as we were preparing for our annual "stewardship" drive (which meant asking for money) I challenged our session to take a more biblical approach to the subject. We spent a number of months, both formally and informally, talking about stewardship from a biblical perspective. Three of our elders volunteered to put together a package of materials that would have the emphasis we had been speaking about. I must admit that I wondered about the outcome. When they presented the results of their several months of work, I was truly amazed. They had come up with an approach that was biblical in every sense of the word. It was also extremely practical. It was far better than anything I could have produced.

Their packet of materials was composed of four separate documents. A cover letter defined stewardship and offered a challenge to make a pledge, not merely of money, but of time and talents as well. A second part of the package was a data form that asked for the usual vital statistics (name, address, phone number) that churches collect. However, it also requested that each person complete what was called a "Christian Service Inventory." Under eight broad categories and almost 100 more specific sub-categories each member was able to check his or her own interests and/or talents. Since it was recognized that some category might have been missed, space was provided for the respondent to indicate other possible areas of interest.

The largest document in the package was a thirteen-page booklet that listed every possible form of worship, study, or service opportunity available to members of our church. Keyed to this by page number was a fourth sheet, entitled "Commitment Opportunities Work-sheet." Each person was encouraged to complete this worksheet and, on the basis of it, make a pledge of a specific number of hours in each of the three categories of worship, study, and service.

This program was presented to the congregation at the time of the annual pledge campaign. For the first time in the history of our church, the stewardship campaign was truly that.

The forms were sent by mail to each member and to nonmembers who requested them. Announcements were made in church and were followed up by telephone calls.

The value of this approach is seen in the fact that these materials are still being used in our new members' classes. When we ask those joining our church to make a financial pledge, we also ask them to commit themselves to a pledge of their time and talents.

Now, on to the matter of finances. At the outset I want to make the blanket statement that raising money is easy. My personal experience supports this. You may remember that in chapter 1 it is noted that the annual budget in my present church has gone from $24,000 to approximately $300,000 in a period of just seventeen years. Our 600-member congregation has supported this budget while just recently committing itself to a building program of approximately $1,500,000.

Raising money is easy if approached in the

right way. Conducting a successful budget campaign by direct mail is really quite simple.

If your church has been in the habit of using the every-member canvass approach to fund raising, about one month prior to your stewardship campaign you should announce to your congregation that visits will not be made this year but that contacts will be made primarily by mail.

One week later—three weeks before pledge cards are to be returned—a mailing consisting of six enclosures should be sent to each member and to the nonmembers who indicate a desire to support the church through the pledge system.

The first piece of the six in the package is a cover letter from the chairperson of the stewardship campaign. This letter should explain the change from the every-member canvass approach to a direct mail approach. It should also describe the other enclosures and encourage the response of the congregation.

It is important to indicate the date by which pledge cards should be returned. The great majority of members will return the cards on or before the date indicated.

One other very important paragraph in this letter should be addressed to the group within every church who consistently refuse to pledge. These people should be asked to return their cards marked, "Do not wish to pledge." The reason for this will become clear later.

A second enclosure should outline the proposed budget for which funds are being raised. Use imagination and ingenuity in preparing this piece. Utilize charts, graphs, humorous line drawings, a variety of typestyles, imaginative copy, and so on. This should be so attractively done that no one will put it down until they have at least glanced through it. If your church has an indebtedness, it is good to indicate this in this enclosure. This information should be as complete and up-to-date as possible. Indicate the reason(s) for the indebtedness, the initial amount, the outstanding debt, and the amount of the monthly payment. This will give every member a good picture of the financial condition of the church and will show quite clearly that the church cannot operate if its members give only $1.00, $2.00, or even $5.00 per week.

The third piece in this packet should be a sheet containing a stewardship report of the past year, indicating the pattern of giving within the congregation. For example:

2 families are giving more than $125.00 per week.
5 families are giving $75.00 to $125.00 per week.

10 families are giving $50.00 to $74.99 per week.

28 families are giving $30.00 to $49.99 per week.

This breakdown will, of course, be governed by the pattern of giving in your particular congregation. The purpose of this report is to show the members of the congregation what others are giving and to encourage each one to step up his or her pledge.

The fourth enclosure is, in some respects, the most important of all. It is an explanation of the reasons for an increase in the budget. On this sheet all new and/or important programs should be explained *in full*.

The last two enclosures are a pledge card and a return envelope with the church's address printed on it. The best color for both of these is bright pink; statistics show that this color, above all others, produces the best return. Why this is the case is unknown, but it does work.

Following the date requested for the return of the pledge cards, a phone call should be made to those whose pledge cards have not yet been returned. Those whose cards are marked "Do not wish to pledge" should not be called. For budgeting purposes, however, assume that the future contributions of these people will remain the same as they have been for the past year.

When the results of the campaign are known, another letter reporting the results and thanking the congregation for their response should be sent to the entire membership. This will serve as a gentle reminder to those who have been called but still haven't returned their cards.

Tithing

In all of the churches I have served, I have emphasized tithing. In my present church, I immediately began to emphasize this biblical approach to financing the church. One year, however, it struck me that my many references to tithing could be supported by a direct mail campaign.

What we called the "Tithing Fellowship" was born. A logo consisting of a large percent sign (%) with a smiling face drawn into the upper circle of the sign was used on each letterhead, along with an appeal to each member to become part of this fellowship. There were no membership cards or meetings. Those who belonged to the fellowship were known only to God.

One month prior to sending the stewardship packet previously described, a series of three "Tithing Fellowship" letters was sent. In the first letter, the congregation was challenged to consider the biblical injunction to tithe and to begin thinking about giving to the Lord's work in terms of percentages, rather than in terms of dollar amounts. The membership was asked to translate the dollar amount of their giving into a percentage of income. They were also asked to consider what percentage of increase it would take each year to be tithing in five years.

The second letter told the story of my family's experience with tithing and asked the members not to dismiss tithing as something totally impractical. It also encouraged them to take their doubts and concerns about tithing to God in prayer.

In the final letter, the reasons for tithing were noted, with emphasis being placed on the fact that tithing benefits the giver in a number of ways. The well known passage from Malachi 3:10 was cited: "Bring the full tithes into the storehouse, that there may be food in my house; and thereby put me to the test, says the Lord of hosts, if I will not open the windows of heaven for you and pour down for you an overflowing blessing."

The results of this campaign were more than gratifying. Over the five-year period needed for the follow through, we saw a number of people join the Tithing Fellowship. Within the next few years, we will probably use this same approach again, since we now have many members who were not a part of our church when it was used before.

Raising money *is* easy—if you ask for it. A direct mail approach makes asking for it easy.

Appendix

Examples of Symmetrical and Optical Balance

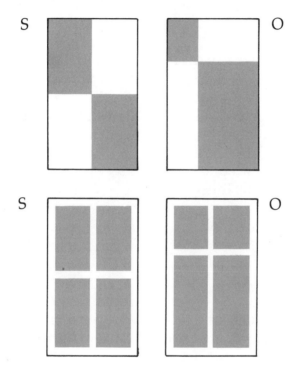

Example of Logo for Men's Letter

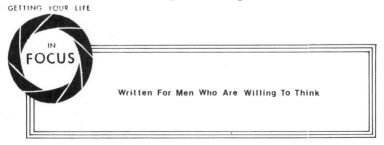

GETTING YOUR LIFE

IN

FOCUS

Written For Men Who Are Willing To Think

New Neighbor Letter #1

Welcome to your new neighborhood!

Ours is an outstanding, friendly community. We are certain that you have already discovered this fact.

We believe that the many fine churches in our area have, to a great measure, influenced the life of our community. By joining one of these churches, you will personally benefit and will help to enlarge the impact they can make on the community at large.

Of course, our hope is that you and your family will find your way to _____ Church. Ours is not a large church, but it is large enough to serve you well and small enough to want to. At _____ Church, we like to think that you are only a stranger until you come through the door; then you become a friend. Ours is a friendly church.

Our main concern is to help people find satisfaction in life through a deep and abiding relationship with Christ.

We welcome you to our community and invite you to attend the services of our church.

New Neighbor Letter #2

A short time ago, we wrote to you about _____ Church.

This letter is to tell you a little bit more about what goes on in our busy life. We think there is something here to appeal to everyone.

Our church is open to everyone who is searching for real meaning in life. Our people have found that this meaning can be discovered in Christ. Ordinary existence becomes LIFE when one is introduced to the Savior.

Why not meet Christ this Sunday morning at _____ Church? We have services at 9:30 and 11:00 A.M. Church school meets at both hours. Adult Bible classes in a variety of formats also meet at both hours. We have vital and active groups for both junior and senior high students. For young adults, there is a college and career age group.

While we emphasize the spiritual, we do not neglect the social needs of people. There are Brownies, Girl Scouts, Boy Scouts, a young people's choir, a children's choir, two bell choirs, a young married couples' fellowship, a singles' group, a women's association, and many other activities too numerous to mention. We have something for YOU.

I look forward to meeting you and getting to know you and your family.

Reading List

The Art of Readable Writing, Rudolph Flesch, Harper & Row, 1960

Better Brochures, Catalogs and Mailing Pieces, Jane Maas, St. Martin's Press, 1981

Editing Your Newsletter: A Guide to Writing, Design and Production, Mark Beach, Coast to Coast Books, 1982

The Elements of Style, William J. Strunk and E. B. White, Macmillan, 1979

Handbook of Effective Church Letters, Stewart Harrel, Abingdon Press, 1965

How to Work with Mailing Lists, Richard Hodgson, Direct Mail/Marketing Assn., 1976

How to Sell Intangibles, Abbott P. Smith, Prentice-Hall, 1958

How to Write Successful Direct Mail Letter Copy, Maxwell C. Ross, Direct Mail/Marketing Assn., 1976

Planning and Creating Better Direct Mail, John D. Yeck, McGraw-Hill, 1961

A Practical Guide to Newsletter Editing and Design, LaRae H. Wales, Iowa State University Press

Promoting Your Cause, Howard Blumenthal, Funk and Wagnalls, 1971

The Solid Gold Mailbox: How to Create Winning Mail Order Campaigns by One Who's Done It All, Walter H. Weintz, Wiley, 1987

Words Ring Louder Than Bells: How to Produce Better Parish Newsletters, Raymond H. Wilson, United Methodist Communications, 1976